Mpuke, Our Little African Cousin

Mary Hazelton Blanchard Wade

Alpha Editions

This edition published in 2023

ISBN : 9789357955904

Design and Setting By
Alpha Editions
www.alphaedis.com
Email - info@alphaedis.com

Contents

Preface

FAR away, toward the other side of the round earth, far to the east and south of America, lies the great continent of Africa. There live many people strange to us, with their black skins, kinky, woolly hair, flat noses, and thick lips. These black people we call Africans or negroes, and it is a little child among them that we are going to visit by and by.

Different as these African people of the negro race are from us, who belong to the white race, they yet belong to the same great family, as we say. Like all the peoples of all the races of men on this big earth, they belong to the human family, or the family of mankind. So we shall call the little black child whom we are going to visit our little black cousin.

We need not go so far away from home, indeed, to see little black children with woolly, kinky hair and flat noses like the little African. In the sunny South of our own land are many negro children as like the little negro cousin in Africa as one pea is like another. Years and years ago slave-ships brought to this country negroes, stolen from their own African homes to be the slaves and servants of the white people here. Now the children and great-grandchildren of these negro slaves are growing up in our country, knowing no other home than this. The home of the great negro race, however, is the wide continent of Africa, with its deserts of hot sand, its parching winds and its tropical forests.

So, as we wish to see a little African cousin in his own African home, we are going to visit little black Mpuke instead of little black Topsy or Sammy, whom we might see nearer by.

It's away, then, to Africa!

CHAPTER I.

THE BOY.

ARE you ready for a long journey this morning? Your eyes look eager for new sights, so we will start at once for Mpuke's strange home. We will travel on the wings of the mind so as to cross the great ocean in the passage of a moment. No seasickness, no expense, and no worry! It is a comfortable way to travel. Do you not think so?

Yes, this is Africa. Men call it the "Dark Continent" because so little has been known of it. Yet it is a very wonderful land, filled with strange animals and queer people, containing the oldest monuments, the greatest desert, the richest diamond mines, in the world.

Some of the wisest people in the world once lived here. Large libraries were gathered together, thousands of years ago, in the cities of this continent.

Yet the little negro whom we visit to-day is of a savage race. He is ignorant of civilised ways and customs. He knows nothing of books and schools. I doubt if he even knows when his birthday draws near; but he is happy as the day is long; his troubles pass as quickly as the April showers.

Let us paint his picture. We must make his eyes very round and bright and black. The teeth should be like the whitest pearls. His head must be covered with a mass of curly black wool. His lips are red and thick, while his skin is black and shining. He is tall and straight, and has muscles of which any boy might well be proud. He is not bothered by stiff collars or tight shoes. He is not obliged to stay in the house when he has torn a hole in his stocking, or ripped his trousers in climbing a tree, because he does not own any of these articles of clothing.

From morning until night, and from night until morning again, he is dressed in the suit Mother Nature provided for him,—his own beautiful glossy skin. She knew well that in the hot land near the equator, where Mpuke was born, he would never feel the need of more covering than this.

One of the first things Mpuke can remember is the daily bath his mother gave him in the river. In the days of his babyhood he did not like it very well, but gave lusty screams when he was suddenly plunged into the cold water. Yet other babies and other mothers were there to keep him company. It is the custom of his village for the women to visit the shore every morning at sunrise to bathe their little ones. What a chattering and screaming there is as one baby after another receives his ducking! Then, spluttering and choking and kicking, he is laid up on the bank to wriggle about on the soft grass, and dry in the sunshine. Now comes a toss upon mother's back, and the procession of women and babies hastens homeward through the shady pathway.

It lies in the very heart of Africa, this home of Mpuke's. The houses are so nearly alike that we almost wonder how the black boy can tell his own from his neighbour's. It can more properly be called a hut than a house. It has low walls made of clay, and a high conical roof thatched with palm leaves. There is not a single window; the narrow doorway faces the one street running through the village. A high wall is built all around the settlement. There are two reasons for this: in the first place, the wild animals must be kept out, and secondly, the village is protected in case another tribe of black people should come to make war upon it. It is sad that it is so, but we know that the negroes spend much of their time in fighting with each other.

There is a small veranda in front of Mpuke's home. It is roofed with the long grasses which are so plentiful in this country, and is a comfortable place for the boy to lie and doze during the hours of the hot midday. The house itself nestles in a grove of banana-trees and stately palms. It makes a beautiful picture. I wish we could take a good painting of it home to our friends.

Look! here comes Mpuke's father. He is the chief of the village, and all the people bow before his greatness and power. We must show proper respect to such an important person, so please don't laugh, although he is certainly an amusing sight.

He is a strong, well-built man, but his body is coloured in such a ridiculous fashion with white and yellow chalk that it reminds us of the clowns at the circus. The braids of wool on his chin look like rats' tails, and others stick out at the sides of his head from under his tall hat of grass. He has a string of charms hanging around his neck; he thinks these will protect him from his enemies, for he is a great warrior. His only clothing is a loin cloth made from the leaves of the pineapple-tree. His good wife wove it for him. His eyebrows are carefully shaved. As he walks along, talking to himself (the negroes are always talking!) he is trying to pull out a hair from his eyelashes with his finger-nail and knife.

This odd-looking man was chosen by the people to be their chief because he is so brave in fighting and so skilful in hunting. He has had many a battle single-handed with an angry elephant or furious panther. He has killed the cobra and the gorilla. He could show you the skulls of the enemies he has slaughtered in battle. He bears many scars beneath that coat of chalk, the marks of dangerous wounds he has received.

Mpuke honours and fears his father, and hopes in his boyish heart that he may grow up to be a chief like him, and have as many daring adventures. His greatest pleasure is in the mock battles which he has with the other boys of the village. Each one must be provided with a wooden spear and a blunt knife before he is ready for the game. Then the boys gather in the open field they use for a playground. This sport is a serious thing; it is a training for the hard fighting which is sure to come later in their lives. The boys rush at each other as if in dead earnest. Hours sometimes pass before either side gains a victory.

CHAPTER II.

BLACKSMITH AND DENTIST.

WHEN the first rays of the morning sun find their way through the tree-tops, the village wakes up. It is the best part of the day in any land, but especially in all tropical countries. The women come hastily out of the doorways, and prepare to get breakfast. All the cooking must be done out-doors, and soon a row of fires can be seen burning brightly in front of the houses. Mpuke's mother is very busy. She must boil the manioc pudding and bake some hippopotamus meat for a hearty meal.

Manioc takes the place of flour with the black man. It looks somewhat like the potato, but the bulbs are not ready to gather till the plant is about fifteen months old. It is a very stringy vegetable. The women gather it in baskets and sink them in the river for a few days. They must stay there until the vegetables have fermented. This fermentation makes them mealy; it also makes it easy to draw out the tough fibres. The manioc is afterward kneaded into dough and made into round puddings, which are boiled several hours.

Mpuke's mother is a careful cook. When her manioc pudding is taken from the fire it is snowy white. It is a wholesome dish, and Mpuke is very fond of it. You may not agree with him unless you like sour milk; for the pudding has a flavour very much like that.

As soon as the meat is cooked, it is cut up and placed in earthen jars, a quantity of pepper is added, and palm oil poured over it to make a rich gravy.

The men eat their breakfast first. When it is finished they sit around under the trees while the women and children satisfy their hunger. The manner in which these people eat is not at all nice, but we must always remember they have never been taught a better way.

There is no table to set; no knives, or forks, or spoons. The savages use only the kind they carry around with them, furnished by Mother Nature when they were born.

They gather around the jars and take out the pieces of meat with their fingers, sopping up the gravy with the manioc bread. Now for some palm wine to quench their thirst. The meal is quickly over. We are glad, for it has not been pleasant to watch.

Both men and women join in a friendly smoke. From the laughing and chattering they must be having a merry time.

But it is growing warm as the sunshine finds its way through the foliage, and there is much work to do before the stifling noon hours.

THE VILLAGE

The women and children hurry away to their plantations of sweet potatoes, or groundnuts (peanuts), or tobacco. Some of the men get their spears and bows and arrows for hunting. Others prepare nets for fishing in the river. Every one is so busy that the village suddenly becomes quiet.

We will follow Mpuke on his way to the blacksmith, who is also the dentist in this little settlement. "What," we say, "is it possible that a savage knows how to fill teeth?" We discover that his work is of a very different kind from that of any dentist we ever met in white man's land. His business is to grind the beautiful white teeth of the people till they are wedge-shaped. Mpuke is going to his hut to-day for this very purpose. His father has a small looking-glass he bought from the white traders, and when Mpuke is a good boy he is allowed to take it and look at himself for a few minutes. He will take great delight in viewing his teeth after they have been ground to the fashionable shape. There is some danger of his growing vain over the compliments he will receive. In the eyes of his own people he is a handsome boy, and needs only the finishing touch to his teeth to make him a beauty.

It is to be hoped that he will not become a dandy when he grows up. His mind, however, is very busy in thinking of warfare and hunting, and he is inclined to scorn the men who think too much of their looks.

See! There is one of the village dandies, now. He is strutting along like a peacock, and expects every one to stop and look at him. He has spent a long time in plastering his hair with clay well mixed with palm oil. The oil is fairly dripping from his face and neck now. We certainly can't admire this style of beauty, so we will turn our attention to the hut on the other side of the road.

The man in the doorway is busy at his work. He is shaping jars and dishes out of clay. Some of the jars are beautiful in shape. Wouldn't you like to buy one of them? A few beads or a bit of bright calico would pay him well, according to his ideas.

Hark! There is the sound of a hammer. Let us take a peep inside of this next hut; we must discover what is being done here. A metal-worker is making armlets and anklets of copper. They will find a ready sale in the village, for no woman considers herself well-dressed unless she is able to wear a number of such ornaments. She is willing to work very hard on the plantation if she can earn enough jewelry to make a rattling noise and a fine display as she walks along.

CHAPTER III.

WORK AND PLAY.

THE dentist works steadily for an hour or so upon Mpuke's teeth; but he grows warm and tired, and says he has done enough filing for one morning. The boy has been very patient and has not uttered a sound of complaint during the painful operation. But now he is delighted to be free, and hurries off to the shore of the river to work on the canoe he is building. His father helped him cut down a large tree, but he is doing all the rest of the work alone. He has worked many days in hollowing out the trunk of the tree. He has shaped it into a narrow, flat-bottomed boat. The paddles are beautifully carved, and there is very little left to be done now except the making of the sail.

That is easy work. The long grasses are already gathered, and he sits on the bank of the river weaving them into a large, firm mat. This will serve as well as canvas for the sail.

What pleasure he will take in this canoe! Many a day he will spend in it, sailing along under the shade of the tall trees which line the river's banks. Many a fish he will catch and bring to his mother for the next meal. He delights in the sport, and does not seem to mind the myriads of gnats and mosquitoes which would send us home in a hurry.

But the black boy's life is not all play. He has had regular work to perform from the time when he began to walk alone. He must learn to make the rattan war shields, shape spears for battle, and weave nets for trapping fish and game. In fact, Mpuke must be ready to help his elders in all their occupations.

The boy has a sister who is nine years old. She looks very much like her brother, and has the same happy disposition. She has many duties, but they are quite different from her brother's.

She is a good cook, young as she is. She can broil a buffalo steak to perfection; it is her work to gather the insects and caterpillars which are considered dainties at the feasts of the black people. She weaves the mats on which the family sleep at night. She helps her mother raise the tobacco, and gathers the peanuts and stores them away for the rainy season.

But let us go back to the river, where Mpuke is giving the finishing touch to his sail. As he turns his head to get a cooling breeze, it brings to his nostrils the smell of the dinner cooking in the village. He knows he must not be late at meal-time, and, besides, he has a good appetite for each of the day's three hearty meals.

He hurries down the path, thinking of the favourite dish his mother has promised him to-day. Do you care to taste it? It is boiled crocodile. The broth is seasoned with lemon juice and Cayenne pepper. "How kind my mother is," thinks Mpuke, "to cook such savoury messes. There are few boys so fortunate as I am. I will try to be a good son, and, if the white traders ever come this way again, I will buy her a chain of beads long enough to wind three times around her neck."

With these thoughts the boy reaches home, but the whole village is in a state of much excitement; great news has just been brought by one of the men. He has discovered a herd of elephants feeding in a forest swamp only a few miles distant. He says that he counted at least a hundred of them.

The black people know that the elephant's sleeping time is from about eleven in the morning till three or four in the afternoon. It is the time that the people themselves take for rest; but to-day there is no noonday nap for Mpuke's village.

Dinner is eaten in haste. The men rush in and out of the houses getting their spears, bows, and poisoned arrows in readiness. The chief orders his assistants to get out his treasured elephant gun. It is the most valuable possession in the village. A small fortune (as the black people count) was given for it to the white traders. The chief's eyes shine, as he says to himself: "This shall bring down an elephant to-day."

CHAPTER IV.

THE ELEPHANT HUNT.

MPUKE is wildly delighted when he finds that he may go on the hunt. But he is warned to be very quiet; he must not even whisper as the party creeps through the dense forest.

HUNTING ELEPHANTS

The hunt will be a failure unless the elephants are taken by surprise while they are sleeping. The men know that the wind is in their favour, since it is blowing from the elephants toward them. Otherwise, the keen-scented creatures would quickly discover the approach of their enemies.

Listen! do you hear that queer noise? It is the champing sound the elephants make in their throats when they are asleep. The hunters creep nearer and nearer; more and more and more carefully, if possible, they turn aside the thick undergrowth of trees and bushes. Ah! Mpuke's father is within a dozen yards of the herd. He looks keenly about till he discovers a huge tusker; he gives a signal to two of his followers to bring up the gun. It is carefully placed and aimed at a spot in the elephant's forehead about four inches above the eyes. It is a vital spot. Two of the best marksmen of the party direct their poisoned arrows at the heart. If all succeed in reaching the parts aimed at there will be nothing to fear. But if the huge creature is only slightly wounded, woe to Mpuke and this company of men who are taking their lives in their hands at this moment! A maddened elephant is a fearful creature to encounter.

Hush! Steady now! Bang! sounds the gun. At the same moment the arrows are let loose from the bows. The bullet was aimed well. It enters the exact spot intended. The arrows do their work. The king of the forest rolls over on his side without a sound. There is not even a death struggle, but there is a sudden commotion among the rest of the herd; it is as though a whirlwind had arisen. Every animal is instantly awake; the herd closes together like a great army. There is an angry uproar, a tremendous trumpeting and bellowing; the forest echoes and re-echoes with the sound. The ground shakes beneath their feet. Madly plunging through the forest, the elephants flee in an opposite direction from the men. As they rush onward, great limbs of trees are torn off as though they were only straws.

Suppose they had turned toward the hunters, instead of from them! It is useless to think of it,—for this time, at least, no one has been harmed. And now the men gather around their prey lying lifeless on the ground.

"Owi?" ("Is it dead?") Mpuke anxiously whispers. His father assures him of the fact, and allows the boy to take part in cutting the flesh away from the monstrous prize.

In a few moments the women of the village appear, carrying baskets. They have followed the party at a distance; they knew their help would be needed if any prey were secured.

The hunt has been a marvellous success. It often happens that hunters are obliged to wait in the underbrush for hours before they can get near enough for a good shot, or to gain such a position as to be able to cut the sinews of the sleeping elephant's legs with their spears, for this makes the animal helpless.

But the safest and most common way of hunting elephants is to dig immense pits near their feeding-grounds. These are covered over with branches. The unwary elephant who comes this way makes a false step, and falls helpless into the pit. It is an easy matter then for the men to approach and kill him, either with their spears or bows and arrows.

But we must turn again to Mpuke and his companions. It is not long before the busy workers have removed all the flesh, and packed it in the big baskets. The monstrous ears must be saved; they will be useful to take the place of carts in harvest time. Two of the strongest men are loaded with the ivory tusks; they must be kept to sell to the traders.

The party hurries homeward, chattering in childish delight over the fun they will have this evening. They leave behind them only the skeleton of the huge animal which two hours since was so powerful.

As soon as they reach the village the boys are put to work. They must dig a pit, and bring wood to fill it. A fire must be kindled and kept burning till the sides of this earthen oven are thoroughly heated. After this the fire is put out, and one of the elephant's legs is laid in the oven.

The women bring green wood and fresh grass to lay over the roast, after which the hole is plastered tightly with mud. But the queer oven is not yet closed tightly enough. The loose earth taken from the pit is piled high above it, so that no heat can possibly escape.

You wonder how long the people must wait before their roast can be served. It will be a day and a half, at least; but when the time does come to open the pit the cooks will find enough tender, juicy meat to furnish every one in the village with a hearty meal.

The leg of an elephant is the most eatable portion of the animal; the rest of the flesh is tough and fibrous, although the negroes eat it, and enjoy it very much. The women smoke it, much as our people smoke ham, and in this way they can keep it a long time for use.

CHAPTER V.

SONG AND STORY.

IT has been a busy day for every one. In the short twilight the people gather about under the trees for music and story-telling. Mpuke runs to his house for his xylophone, and begins to play a sweet, sad air. One by one his neighbours join in an accompaniment with their rich voices. The African is a natural lover of music; he uses it to express all his feelings.

It is a weird sight,—this group of black people rocking their bodies to and fro to keep time with the music. As they enter more deeply into the spirit of the evening song the expressions of their faces change; they seem to forget themselves, and become a part of the music itself.

And now the frogs add their voices to the chorus. The crickets and cicadas pipe their shrill notes, while at short intervals a hoarse sound, between a groan and a whining bark, is wafted upwards from the river. It comes from a lonely crocodile who, no doubt, would like to join the company. It is much better for their comfort that he remains where he is.

Mpuke's xylophone is made of strips of soft wood, differing in length, fastened over a set of calabashes. In each calabash a hole has been carefully bored and covered over with spider's web. Perhaps you mistook the calabash for a gourd, which looks much like it. It is a curious growth which forms on the trunks of certain trees near Mpuke's home.

Our little friend makes sweet liquid music on his crude instrument. He calls it a marimba. The village metal-worker made it for the boy in return for many presents of fish.

"That is a good lad," said the man, "he is thoughtful and generous. I will make him happy."

After the people have finished their songs, there is music on other instruments besides Mpuke's. Look at that big fellow blowing into an ivory horn. He needs to have a strong pair of lungs if he is going to continue very long. What a dirge-like noise he makes! But when the tom-tom begins to sound, everybody is roused and joins in a wild dance.

The people wind in and out among the trees, round and round again, laughing, shouting, and singing, until they sink out of breath on the grass.

Mpuke is so tired he can hardly keep his eyes open. He drags himself into the hut where his sister lies on her mat, already sound asleep. Listen! what is that scuttling noise among the dried leaves in the corner? Mpuke's bright black eyes are helped by the moonlight streaming through the doorway. He discovers that it is a green lizard, which he knows to be quite harmless. But it is always wise to be watchful.

One night, not many moons ago, as the black boy counts time, he found a centipede close to his bare feet when he woke up suddenly in the night. He is quite sure that a good spirit roused him to save his life.

At another time a lizard of the most deadly kind must have shared the boy's mat with him through the night. At any rate, he found the lizard at his side when his eyes opened to the morning light.

But Mpuke is too sleepy to think about unpleasant things, and in another moment he is dreaming of the roasted elephant that will make to-morrow's feast.

A week passes by. We will visit Mpuke once more as he is eating his early breakfast.

A messenger from the next village comes rushing in to the people. He has run ten miles this morning through the forest paths, and has brought word to Mpuke's father from his own chief. The two men are blood-brothers, and have promised to stand by each other in all troubles and dangers. "Blood-brothers," you say, "what does that mean?" When the chiefs were only boys they went through a sacred ceremony together. An arm of each was cut till the blood ran, then the two arms were pressed together, and the blood was allowed to mingle.

They must never quarrel again. No cruel words or deeds should ever pass between them, because they are now bound together by the strongest of all ties.

But what is the message that causes such a state of excitement? It tells that enemies are approaching. It means war, and preparation for awful deeds. Mpuke's father is asked to come to the help of his blood-brother. Will he join him to meet the advancing foes?

There is only one answer possible; not a moment must be lost. The order is given to sound the war-drums; the people burst into an exciting battle-song; blasts from ivory trumpets can be heard throughout the village; the men cover their faces with charcoal and hastily seek the medicine-man. He must provide them with charms to protect them from danger. Poor fellow, he is the busiest one of all the people, making little packages of beads, shells, and stones for each soldier to wear as a talisman.

The women are at work getting the spears and arrows together; they must also sharpen the knives for their husbands and sons.

These ignorant savages make a hideous sight to our eyes when the fury of war seizes them. It is such a pitiful thing that they are ready to take the lives of their brother blacks for the slightest reason, and that they delight so greatly in war.

Now the men hurry down to the river's side. They jump into their canoes, and are out of sight as soon as they pass a bend in the banks of the stream. Mpuke watches them with glistening eyes; he longs to follow them, but he has been told to remain at home to protect his mother and sisters in case of danger.

He knows already what war means; it was only last year that his own village was attacked. Young as he was, he stood all day behind the spiked wall, sharpened spear in hand, doing his part to defend his home. He was wounded in the leg on that terrible day, and for a long time afterward lay sick with fever. His sister was so good to him during that trying time; hour after hour she sat at his side on the veranda, and kept the flies and mosquitoes from his wound with a broom she made of an elephant's tail.

Mpuke thinks of this as he goes home through the forest path. Suddenly he stops quite still; his eyes roll in terror. A huge serpent lies coiled but a few feet away; he does not notice Mpuke, for his beadlike eyes are fastened on a monkey standing on the ground in front of him. The snake is charming it. He will force it to its own death, and yet he does not stir; it is the monkey that moves. It comes nearer and nearer to the monster; it makes a frightened cry as it advances.

Mpuke knows he cannot save its life, as he has no weapon with which to attack the serpent. He would like to run, but does not stir until the monkey, having come close to its charmer, is suddenly strangled in the folds of its powerful body. The boy does not wait to see the snake devour his prey, but hurries homeward, without once daring to turn round.

The fires have all been put out. The women and children are talking in whispers. They wish to make as little noise as possible while the men are away, lest they be attacked by wild beasts or some passing band of savages.

Night comes; there is no sound of returning warriors. Mpuke sits in the doorway of his home, listening; his mother and sister are beside him. It draws near midnight, and yet there is no sleep for the anxious watchers.

Hark! faintly at first, then more and more plainly, the fighting song of the returning warriors is borne to them on the evening wind. And now they can hear the sound of paddles and shouts of boisterous laughter.

The men must have been victorious or they would not come home so gaily. There are but a few more minutes of waiting before the black heroes enter the village. We call them heroes, for that is the way their families think of them.

The men are tired, excited, and stained with blood. They are bringing home two of their comrades wounded, and the dead body of another. They have six prisoners taken from the enemy. These poor wretches are bound with ropes; they know their fate too well. They are now slaves, and must hereafter do the hardest work for their new masters.

The customs of their own settlement are different from those of Mpuke's village. They will suffer from homesickness, and will have many new things to which they must get used.

It seems strange to us that in travelling a short distance in the heart of Africa the people are found to differ from each other so much in language, habits, and even dress. For, scanty as it is, the style of decoration of one tribe varies greatly from that of another.

For instance, in Mpuke's home we know it is the fashion to have wedge-shaped teeth, while not far away the people think that a really beautiful person must have the teeth pointed. In one village the women wear wooden skewers pierced through their noses; in another, their principal ornaments consist of metal rings in the ears, and metal armlets, anklets, and bracelets.

Among some tribes, the men's hair is braided in queer little tails, while others have it knotted at the back of the head and at the chin in tight bunches.

CHAPTER VI.

THE BATTLE FEAST.

IT is the day after the battle. Mpuke's father orders his people to celebrate the victory. He tells them to prepare a great feast, as his blood-brother, Ncossi, is invited to come and bring his people.

"HIS FOLLOWERS LOOK UPON HIM WITH THE GREATEST ADMIRATION"

A great deal of work must be done before the feast is ready. Some of the villagers prepare their nets to catch a certain fish that is rare and delicate. Others get their canoes ready for a hippopotamus hunt; still others search for young monkeys. They must also get a kind of snake that makes a delicious stew.

The children are sent through the fields and woods to gather the rarest and choicest insects. The country is scoured in all directions. The feast will surely be "fit for a king," at least an African king.

The great day comes at last, and the chief Ncossi arrives. He is dressed in the greatest splendour. A chain of leopards' teeth is wound around his neck; a great war knife hangs at his side. One of his cheeks is painted red and the other yellow. The heads of wild animals are tattooed upon his arms. He wears on his head a tall, tattered, beaver hat, for which he must have paid a great price to some trader. He is a hideous object, yet, as he struts along, his followers look upon him with the greatest admiration, and keep exclaiming: "Look at our beautiful chief! Look at our beautiful chief!"

The mouths of the visitors water as they behold the pots boiling over the great fires, and the savoury odours of the meats greet their nostrils.

How glad they are that they have been invited to the fine banquet promised here! They act like happy children out for a holiday. There is no sign in their faces of the cruel side of their natures which showed itself in the battle a few days ago.

And now they gather in a circle on the grass, and begin to devour the good things the cooks spread before them.

Will you share with them this dish of boiled smoked elephant? It is coarse and stringy; I fear you will not care for a second piece, although every one pronounces it delicious. The roasted monkey is fat and tender. You will enjoy it more if you do not allow yourself to think of its resemblance to a baby. The stewed buffalo ribs served with lemon juice and Cayenne pepper are fine, while we should not disdain the turtle soup if it were brought us in the best hotel in America.

The side dishes at this feast are the queerest we have ever seen,—frizzled caterpillars, paste of mashed ants, and toasted crickets. Palm oil has been freely used in the crocodile stew and elephant gravy.

Mpuke's friends and relatives are enjoying themselves hugely. They gobble the good things in the most remarkable manner. They are so busy that they are almost silent. They drink large quantities of palm wine as well as the fermented juice of the baobab-tree. Palm wine is very pleasant and refreshing when it is first made. To-morrow, after the visitors have left, Mpuke will show us how to obtain it. He is an obliging little fellow, and will willingly climb a tall palm-tree to the very top, bore deep holes in the wood, and fasten gourds into which the juice will drip. We should drink it at once, before it changes into the sour, intoxicating liquor drunk so freely at the feast.

Not many days after the celebration, the rainy season began. During this period the rain does not fall all day long, but comes down in torrents for an hour or two every morning.

Very little hunting is done now, but there are such good supplies of smoked elephant and buffalo meat it is not necessary.

Mpuke wakes up one morning with great pain in his head, and it does not go away after he gets up. He says to himself, "I am afraid some bad spirit bewitched me while I was dreaming last night." But he says nothing about his bad feelings to his mother. He is afraid she will think of the sleeping sickness. He does not want her to worry, so he will wait awhile and perhaps the pain will go away.

The sleeping sickness is the most terrible visitor in an African home. There is little hope for the one who has it. Sometimes the sufferer is ill for a few weeks only, but again he may linger for a year before death comes.

The illness begins with a severe headache; next comes swelling of the body, like dropsy; in the last stage, the dying person dozes or sleeps all of the time.

With our little Mpuke, a day and a night pass and his headache grows worse and worse. His body is first hot and feverish, then shivering with a chill. His mother begins to notice how slowly he moves, and how hard it seems for him to do his work.

"You must lie on your mat in the hut, my dear one," she says to the boy. "The charm doctor shall be sent for; he will drive away the evil spirit that is making my child so sick."

The black woman has a strange belief; she thinks that evil beings are always near, ready to work harm. She spends much time in protecting her family and herself from these evil powers by repeating charms and going through queer ceremonies.

She teaches her children to fear spirits in the air, in the water, in the trees, in the ground; at every movement they look for possible trouble from beings they cannot see, yet imagine to be following them. If it were not for such a foolish belief, the black people would be very happy; but they have one protector to whom they turn in all their troubles. They believe that he can drive away the evil spirits; he can bring health to the sick man; he can make charms to ward off the attacks of wild beasts; he can even control the winds and the waters.

CHAPTER VII.

THE AFRICAN MEDICINE-MAN.

WHEN the crops begin to dry up, it is the medicine-man who has the power to bring rain; when fever visits the settlement, his herbs and charms are alone of any use in relieving suffering. Therefore, when Mpuke becomes ill, the medicine-man is immediately visited.

His hut stands a little apart from the others in the village. It is very seldom that an outsider is allowed to enter the sacred (?) place. After Mpuke's mother has wrapped up her little son, and placed him on his mat, she hastens to the home of the charm doctor, carrying an offering of tobacco and palm wine to the great man.

As she draws near the hut, he appears in the doorway. He wears many chains of metal rings about his body. Funny little packages are tied to the rings, and are supposed to possess the power of working wonders. Feathers of different kinds of birds are sticking out of the packages, while a doleful clanging is made by iron bells at every movement of the "doctor."

When told of Mpuke's sickness, he goes back into the hut and puts on his tall hat of panther's skin. He takes some herbs and wonder-working charms from a dark corner, and comes out looking very solemn and quiet. He rarely speaks to Mpuke's mother as she reverently follows him to her own home.

In a few moments he is standing by the black boy's side. He makes some weird and mysterious motions, and tells Mpuke that he is driving away the evil spirit that has taken hold of his body. He gives the anxious mother a charm made from the hairs of an elephant's tail; this is to be fastened around the boy's neck. She is told to repeat certain words many times a day, and to draw a circle with ashes around the hut to keep bad spirits from returning.

But this is not all that is to be done for the cure of the boy; for the doctor really does know many good uses of herbs. He has discovered that the use of one of these is almost sure to break up a fever like Mpuke's, so he steeps a large dose of this medicine, to be taken during the next three days. Then he goes away as quietly and solemnly as he came; the villagers bow before him in awe as they pass him on his way.

Mpuke is soon strong and well. What cured him? Did the doctor really have the power to drive spirits away? Or was it the medicine the boy swallowed? Of course, his mother believes nothing could have been done without the magic charms, but those who are wise must see that if the herb tea had not been made and swallowed, Mpuke would most likely be still burning with fever.

But Mpuke is now well and strong, glad to be out once more in his canoe; eager to look for honey in the wild bees' nests; chasing the monkeys from the banana-trees; feeding his chickens, and doing a hundred other things beside all these.

But the chickens we hardly recognise as such, they are such poor, scrawny things, with their bodies and feathers all awry; and when Mpuke's mother prepares a chicken stew, the meat is so dry and tasteless that it seems scarcely worth eating. What can be the reason that the African chicken is so much poorer than the American bird? Perhaps it is because it is tormented by such numbers of insects.

This reminds me of something that once happened at Mpuke's home. One night, in the midst of sound sleep, they were suddenly attacked by an army. There were millions, yes, billions, in that army, yet it made no sound as it drew near. It had travelled many miles through fields and forests, and Mpuke's home happened to be in the line of march. That is the reason it was attacked.

For a few moments the sleepers were in a state of great excitement. There was much scuffling, screaming, scratching, and running about. Then all was quiet once more, and the family returned to their mats and dreams.

The strange army was not one of human beings, but, nevertheless, it caused fear and trembling while it stayed. It was composed of ants, much larger than any we have ever seen in our own country. They were under the orders of generals who marched at the sides of the advancing columns. Each ant knew his place and duty. He was ready to bite any living creature that barred his way; and it was a fierce bite, too, for a piece of flesh was taken out each time before he let go.

For some reason unknown to us, the ants were changing their camping-ground and moving to another part of the forest. Such a small thing as Mpuke's home must not be allowed to stand in their way, so they passed through it, and took the people inside by surprise.

"Ouch!" screamed Mpuke, as he woke up to find himself covered by these wise but uncomfortable insects. Then, one after another, the boy's father, that brave warrior, his mother, his sister, and himself, fled from the hut as though a pack of hyenas were after them.

When morning came the ants had departed, but not an insect was left alive in the house. The fat spiders that had spun comfortable webs in the dark corners were now skeletons, a baby lizard lay lifeless in the doorway, and many crickets had fallen victims to the resistless invaders. Worse still! when Mpuke looked for his pet chicken, nothing was left of it save bones and feathers.

Paul Du Chaillu, an African explorer, has written very interesting accounts of the ants found in that country. The wisdom of these little creatures fills us with wonder. Small as they are, they travel in such numbers that even the wild beasts of the forest hasten to get out of their way. They are not fond of the sunlight, and when marching in the day-time they prefer to stop in their journey and dig a tunnel underground rather than pass over an open plain.

CHAPTER VIII.

THE GORILLA.

BUT we will leave the ants and their wonderful ways for the present, as we wish to follow Mpuke, whose mother has sent him a long way from home to gather some pineapples. The boy's sister carries a large basket on her head to hold the fruit. Pineapples allowed to ripen fully where they grow are much nicer than those picked while still a little green in order to stand the long journey to us. They are so tender that when Mpuke has cut off the top of one he can scoop out the pulp and eat it as though it were oatmeal porridge. And it is so sweet and juicy! It is no wonder the children were glad to go on their errand.

They play hide and seek among the bushes as they run along; they laugh and chatter and joke without a thought of fear, they are so used to the forest. Besides, Mpuke carries a bow and arrow in his hand to be ready in case of need.

They soon reach the place, but discover that some one has been there before them. The fruit lies scattered over the ground. The children look about them in alarm; they speak in low tones instead of the noisy chatter of the moment before.

"Mpuke, do you think a gorilla is near us?" whispers his sister, and the next instant there is a loud crackling and trampling of the bushes.

Ten yards away stands the fiercest, wildest looking creature one can imagine. She is covered with dark, almost black, hair; standing on her short hind legs she is taller than most human beings.

How long her arms look, as she beats her breast in anguish! She does not notice the children hiding behind the trunk of a tree. She is looking down on the ground where her dead baby is lying. Has a passing hunter shot it during its mother's absence, or did it sicken and die? We do not know; we can only listen, breathless, to the mother's cry, too horrible to be described. See! she lifts the dead body in her arms and moves away.

When travellers in the Dark Continent first brought home accounts of this largest and most fearful of the ape family, people could scarcely believe in the truth of their statements, but now every one admits the gorilla to be the king of the African forest.

As soon as the frightened children reach home and tell their adventure, a party of the best huntsmen starts into the forests. If there is one gorilla in the neighbourhood, there must be more. No fruit is safe now; the village itself is not secure so long as the dreaded brutes are near. Besides these reasons for killing them, the people consider the brain of a gorilla the most powerful charm that can be used against one's enemies.

While the hunters are gone, we will listen to a legend Mpuke's mother is telling her children. It shows how the power of a man's mind can conquer even the strength of a gorilla.

HOW THE GORILLA CAME.

My children, this is a story of a far-distant tribe of our race. It was told me by my mother, and she in turn listened to it at her mother's knee. I cannot tell you how old it is, but it is very ancient.

Once upon a time there was a certain king who was very rich and powerful. He had many children, but they were all daughters, and this made him feel exceedingly sad. He longed for a son to take his place when he should die. At length, after many years, he was delighted at the birth of a baby boy.

The child grew rapidly into a strong, bright little fellow, and the king's heart was wrapped up in him. His father strove to gratify his smallest wish, and even divided with him his power over the kingdom. Of course the boy became proud and vain. He was quite spoiled by the flattery of his subjects and his father's lavish presents.

One day, as he was sitting under a tree with a circle of youths about him, he said:

"Oh, how fortunate a boy I am; there is nothing my father would refuse to give me. There is not another youth in the world like me!"

He had no sooner finished speaking than one of his boy subjects dared to make answer: "Sir Prince, there is one thing your father would refuse to give you, if you should ask for it, because he could not do it."

"What do you mean?" asked the proud prince, indignantly.

"It is the moon," was the answer.

The young prince went at once to the king and said: "My dear father, you have never in my life refused me anything, and yet I have even now been taunted that if I were to ask it, you would not be able to get the moon for me. Must I endure this? Say that you will obtain it."

The king was troubled. It seemed that it would be impossible for him to satisfy his child for the first time, and he could not bear it. He sent criers throughout the country to call the wise men of his kingdom together, that he might ask their advice.

When they were all assembled, and heard that the king desired them to find a way by which the moon might be brought down to the prince, they, too, were troubled. They feared the king was going crazy; at least all of the wise men but the one who seemed to be the youngest. He turned to the king and slowly said:

"O King, there is a way by which this thing may be done, but it requires long and great work. All the men of the country will be needed in cutting down the forest and shaping timber. All the women will be needed to plant the gardens, raise crops, and cook food for the men. All the children will be needed to make bark rope to tie the timbers in place, and to hand things to the builders. For, O King, this is my plan:

"Yonder mountain is very high, and I propose that a scaffold be built to cover its entire top; that a smaller scaffold be built on that; a still smaller, on that; and so on, until the moon is reached. Then it can be lifted down and brought to your son."

The king did not hesitate as to what he should do. He began at once to act upon the wise man's plan.

All the men in the country went to work cutting down the forest and putting up the scaffold. All the women set to work to cook for the workmen and to plant new gardens. All the children were kept busy making the bark rope and in running errands for their parents.

A month passed; the first scaffold had been built, and yet another upon that.

Two months,—and now the top of the tower could no longer be seen by the multitude at the foot, for the people of all the countries round about had gathered there to watch the strange work.

Three months, four months, five months were gone, and the head workmen sent word down that now the moon was within easy reach.

At last it was whispered that the king, who had climbed to the top, was about to seize the moon and bring it down to earth. More people, from still greater distances, gathered at the foot to behold the great event.

What happened, my children? At first the moon could not be budged from its place; but then more force was applied. Lo! there was a cracking and snapping, as of a tremendous explosion. A river of fire came flowing down the scaffolds, which were quickly burned, together with all the people upon them, and most of those gathered at the foot of the mountain.

Most wonderful of all, those few grown people who did escape were changed into gorillas, while the children that were saved were transformed into monkeys.

My children, when you look at the moon on bright nights, you will notice dark spots upon it, where the shoulders of the strong man who tried to move it from its place were pressed against it.

Let this lesson be learned from my story: It is not well to gratify all the wishes of children; but only such as the parents think wise and good for them.

CHAPTER IX.

THE GORILLA HUNT.

AFTER many hours the hunters return. They have a wonderful tale to tell of what they have seen and done. Mpuke's father is the story-teller. The black faces of the listeners are very still, and all eyes are turned toward him as he speaks. He says:

"My people, we hunters went away from this village very quietly, as you all know. We did not wish the creatures of the forest to hear us as we crept along, one behind another. Our enemies, the gorillas, must not learn of our approach.

"We went on and on, farther and farther to the east. There was no path; we broke off twigs and leaves from the trees and scattered them along on the ground, so we should be able to find our way home again."

Here the whites of the chief's eyes grew larger and rounder as he rolled them about in his head, and looked from one to another of his listeners. Then he continued:

"As we moved on through the forest, we stopped from time to time to listen. But there was no sound of the great gorillas' feet stamping upon the ground. There was no shaking of the limbs of trees. They could not be there.

"At last we came out of the forest into a wooded marsh. The mud was so deep that our feet sank far in at every step. It was a very bad place for us if we should need to run, but it was the very spot gorillas would like if they were in search of dinner, for there were great numbers of bushes loaded with berries, of which, you know, the fierce gorilla is very fond, as well as of other fruits and nuts.

"Hark! there was a sound of tramping feet. The ground trembled, and straight ahead of me I counted one, two, three full-grown gorillas. Two of their children were following them. They were moving along through an open space in the bog. Now they went on all fours, and again they would raise their great bodies and walk along, even as we do ourselves.

"HE SAT DOWN ON HIS HAUNCHES"

"They looked around, now and then, turning their ugly, wrinkled faces toward me, but they had not discovered us. How sharp and wicked their eyes were! What long and powerful arms they had! They stopped beside the bushes and began to eat the berries.

"Mpuke, you would have enjoyed watching a mother gorilla feed her child. She would pick a berry, and then make a queer kind of chuckle to call her little one. He would run to her, and spring up into her arms. She would show her love by moving her thin black hand over his body, and pressing him to her breast. Then down he would jump again, or squat between her legs, while she picked more berries and handed them to him.

"Oh, those gorillas are strange and fearful creatures! But the time had come to let them know we were near by. Bang! went my gun, and the shot went straight into the breast of the mother gorilla. She fell over on her side, with a sharp cry. All the rest fled among the trees except a father gorilla, who rose up on his hind legs. At the same time he gave a fearful roar, and beat his breast, as though he were daring us to attack him. Before he had a chance to spring among us, whizz! flew the arrows from the bows of our brave hunters, and a moment after he lay lifeless on the ground.

"We waited a long time in the place, hoping the other gorillas would come back, but not a single one appeared. The sun was getting low in the sky, so we started homeward. It would not be wise to stay in that damp, wild place after dark.

"We returned to the forest, and began to pick out our way. It was hard to find the tracks we had made on our way east. We had not gone far before I saw a dark object moving toward a high tree ahead of us. I gave the sign to halt. Was it another gorilla? No, it was not large enough, and I could see it had a bald, black, shiny head.

"It must be a chimpanzee. He reached the tree and climbed it, hand over hand. When he had found a comfortable crotch, he sat down on his haunches, and put one long arm around a branch of the tree, to hold himself in place. He must have come up here to rest for the night.

"He was just about to close his eyes, when one of our hunters made a slight noise in the bushes. Before we could fire, the startled chimpanzee had sprung from the tree and disappeared into the darkness of the forest. You well know how shy the creatures are. They are not as bold as gorillas, and will never fight if they can avoid doing so.

"But our story is not yet ended. I am very tired. Gombo, will you tell my people what we discovered as we nearly reached the village?"

CHAPTER X.

THE RACE OF DWARFS.

THE great chief leaned back against a tree-trunk, while Gombo went on with the tale of the day's adventures.

He told the astonished company that not a mile away was a camp of the strangest beings his eyes had ever beheld. He had heard of them and their ways from his own parents, but they had never wandered into this part of the country before.

They belonged to the race of dwarfs, and the very tallest one among them was hardly more than four feet high. Their hair grew in little tufts, or bunches, all over their heads; that of the women was no longer than the men's. Their upper lips were thick, and hung out over their mouths. Their skin was a reddish black, and their cheek-bones were high. And the children! They were such tiny, tiny things.

When they saw Mpuke's people, they huddled together like a pack of dogs, and hid their heads. A mother pigmy held a baby. She looked like a child, while it seemed as though the baby must be a doll in her arms.

These queer little people were cutting down branches and making ready to build their huts. The men came out to meet the hunters, carrying tiny bows and arrows. They made signs that they would like to become friends. They had heard of the banana plantation in Mpuke's village. They were willing to help the chief in his wars and catch game for his people if they could be paid in bananas.

Do you suppose the black hunters laughed at the idea of help from this group of tiny people? Indeed not. They had heard many stories of the great skill of the dwarfs with the bow and arrow, and of their great daring. They had heard, too, how much harm they could do if they took a dislike to a tribe or person. They knew it was wise to make friends with the little people.

Although they were very tired, they joined in a dance to show their good-will. But the pigmies had no music. One of their number beat time by striking a bow with an arrow while the others strutted around in a circle. They looked comical enough, for they kept their legs very stiff and made their faces as solemn as possible. The hunters would have laughed if they dared. It was certainly odd to call that dancing. They pitied the tiny savages, with no musical instruments and no idea of tunes or songs.

CHAPTER XI.

HOW THE DWARFS LIVE.

"HOW do these queer little people sleep?" asks Mpuke, as Gombo stops for a moment in his story. "Don't they have any houses to protect them during the storms? And what kind of clothes do the men and women wear? I don't see that they have a chance to make many things, since they move from place to place so often."

"Dear me," answers the hunter, "you forget, Mpuke, what I said about their house-building when we found them. People of other tribes have told me that their houses are like beehives. They gather long, elastic branches, and bend them over into a curved roof for the house, fastening the ends to the ground. The longest branches are placed over the middle of the house. Shorter ones are laid on each side, and afterward the whole roof is covered with leaves.

"AFTERWARD THE WHOLE ROOF IS COVERED WITH LEAVES"

"The doorway is so low one has to creep into the house on his hands and knees, and all he finds inside is a bed made of sticks. That cannot be very comfortable or soft, can it, Mpuke?

"Their only clothing is an apron of palm leaves, which is very easily made. Oh, these queer little folk have an easy time of it, but I should not wish to live as they do. They have no bread, for they plant no manioc. They keep a fire burning as long as they stay in a place, so they can roast the game they shoot or trap. But that is the only cooking they ever do."

"How do they light their fires?" asks the curious Mpuke.

"They hunt around in the ground till they find two pieces of flint, and strike them together till they get sparks, just as I would myself," the hunter answers.

"Do you think they will steal from us unless we watch carefully?" asks one of the women, anxiously. "If they are thievish, I must hide my ornaments in the ground when we are to be away from the village."

"Do not be afraid," Gombo quickly replies, "for every one says they are very honest, and scorn a theft. To be sure, it would not be a strange thing for a pigmy to shoot his arrow into the centre of a cluster of bananas, as a sign that when it ripens it shall be picked by him alone. But if he should do such a thing he would bring you enough game to pay for it. On the other hand, it would not be well for you to dare to pick a bunch that he has marked in this way, even though it is on your own tree, and he has never asked you for it. He would feel insulted if you should touch it, once he has claimed it for his own.

"These little people are good friends, but bad enemies, and we must show ourselves kind neighbours. As to your bracelets and anklets, you need have no fear whatever. The dwarfs do not seem to care for ornaments. Even their women do not try to look beautiful."

Gombo stops a moment to rest. He notices that the night is growing late. The chief rises and gives a signal for the people to scatter to their homes.

Mpuke is soon in the land of dreams; but he is awake bright and early next morning. He is anxious to visit his new neighbours, and get acquainted with the children of the dwarfs. As soon as his early breakfast is over, the black boy hurries away over the forest path, and soon reaches the camp of the pygmies.

There is a fire in the hollow of a tree-trunk which the children are tending. The men and women are busy making their little huts. There are about thirty people in all. Mpuke makes signs of friendship, and smiles at the boys and girls who are so tiny beside himself. They soon get over their shyness, and show him their bows and arrows. One of the boys is very proud of his skill, and well he may be. Mpuke envies him when he sees him shoot one, two, three arrows in succession, so rapidly that the third one leaves the bow before the first one reaches the mark. Mpuke is a skilful archer, but he cannot shoot as well as the little dwarf.

"How do you fish?" he asks the children. "Do you use nets, or catch the fish with hooks?"

They take their fishing-rods and go down to the river with him. He is very much surprised when he sees them tie pieces of meat on the ends of their lines, and dangle them in the water.

"They must be silly creatures," thinks Mpuke, "to believe they can catch fish in any such way as that."

But he finds they are not silly. They are very skilful little fishermen; they are so clever in their motions, and they give such quick pulls at just the right moment, that they land fish after fish in a few minutes' time.

"I can learn a good many things from the dwarfs," thinks the boy. "I will spend all the time I can with them as long as they stay in this part of the country."

He bids them a pleasant good-bye, and scampers homeward to tell his mother what he has seen. Our little black cousin soon reaches an open space where the trees have been cut down. The grass is high and thick, but he hurries along, trampling it under foot as he makes a path for himself.

CHAPTER XII.

SPIDERS!

SUDDENLY Mpuke has a queer feeling about his bare legs, as though he were caught in a net. Has any one been setting a snare here for birds or rabbits? Surely not, or Mpuke would have heard of it. The boy's bright eyes discover in a flash that he has entered the palace of an immense black and yellow spider. At the moment of discovery he receives a sharp sting on one of his bare legs.

"Ouch! ouch!" he cries, and jumps about in great distress.

Wicked as Mr. Spider looks, his bite is not dangerous, and Mpuke hurries home all the faster now to get some cooling herbs from his mother. They will soon take away the pain, and make the swelling go down.

Mpuke has watched the ways of spiders many times before, but always at a safe distance. This king of spiders spins so strong a web that he can even trap birds in it. He kills them by sucking their blood in the same way he treats his other prey. As for beetles, flies, and wasps, it is mere sport for him to end their lives, once they enter his castle.

It was only last week that Mpuke discovered a spider he had never heard of before. It had its home in a burrow in the earth, shaped like a tunnel. As the boy was lying under a tree, half curled up in the bright sunshine, he saw a spider suddenly appear on the ground near by. It had no web. It seemed as though the earth must have opened to let it out.

Mpuke was wide awake in an instant, for, as you know, he is always ready to learn a lesson from his kind teacher, Mother Nature. He watched the spider disappear into the earth again, at the very spot where it had come out.

"Aha!" said the boy to himself, "I understand now, Mr. Spider. Your home is underground, and you have made a trapdoor that swings as you push it. You have covered it with earth so no one can find out where you live. When you hear a noise of some one coming you creep out upon your prey." At this moment the spider appeared again, and pounced upon a poor clumsy caterpillar who was making his way slowly past his enemy's home. The caterpillar was many times larger than the spider, but what of that? The spider was quick and cunning in his motions; the caterpillar was strong, yet clumsy. There were several minutes of hard fighting, during which the spider gave several sharp bites and drew blood from his enemy. Then, seizing him from behind, he drew him backwards down into his cell below.

Mpuke waited awhile before he dug open the spider's burrow. He found it lying quite still and stupid; the caterpillar was dead and partly eaten. Perhaps the spider felt dull after a big dinner; perhaps he was only startled at having his home suddenly destroyed and laid bare in the sunlight.

Many little gray spiders spin their webs in Mpuke's home, but his mother would not destroy them for the world. They are great helpers in destroying the insects which make it hard to rest comfortably at night. There are ants of different kinds, mosquitoes in abundance, swarms of flies, besides the great African cockroaches that make the walls creak as they travel along their sides.

Mr. Spider is a real friend to the people because he is not afraid of these creatures, although they are his enemies as well as Mpuke's.

The boy sometimes lies in bed and watches the battles fought by the spiders. There is one old fellow whose web is spun near Mpuke's head. He must be quite old, yet he is very quick, and always on the watch for his prey.

"I believe he never sleeps," thinks the boy, "at least I never yet saw his eyes closed. And, oh, my! what an appetite he has; although he eats so much, yet he does not seem to grow any fatter."

Mpuke likes to tell his playmates of the way in which this old gray spider mastered an immense roach. The roach was walking grandly along one day, with no thought of any one interfering with his dignity, when out pounced Mr. Spider from behind and jumped upon his back. It would have been easy enough for the roach to walk off with his enemy, if the spider had not clung with its hairy hind feet to the wall. They seemed to have hooks on the ends and dug into the bark, holding the spider and its prey in the spot where the attack was first made.

Now the battle began in earnest. They fought as fiercely as two panthers. It sometimes seemed as though the roach would win the victory and carry off the spider, but the latter managed to reach over to his enemy's neck and give him a severe bite. The pain must have been great. He grew weaker and weaker, and, after two or three more bites, he gave up the battle. Mr. Spider had won a prize.

Some people say that it will be fair weather to-day because there are so many fresh cobwebs on the grass. They do not know why that is a good sign, but Mpuke knows. He has often watched spiders at work, and seen the half-liquid substance drawn out from tiny tubes in the body. As it reaches the air it hardens into the silk threads which are guided into place by the spider's hind legs. This odd substance is made in an organ called the spinneret, at the very end of the spider's body. He can draw it out as he pleases, but it takes time to make it, so he is never wasteful. He therefore does not spin a web unless he feels quite sure the winds and rains will not spoil it. He has wonderful senses by which he hears and feels things which are not heard or felt by human beings. He rarely makes a mistake in his judgment of the probable weather.

Did you ever see a spider's web propped up by a tiny twig? The threads are quite elastic, and after a time become stretched so that the web sags. Then the clever little workman feels that it can be made to last longer if it is strengthened. He looks around until he discovers the right kind of prop, and puts it into place much as a carpenter straightens a leaning building. The spider has certainly learned many things in Mother Nature's workshop.

But how does Mpuke spend the afternoon after he has returned from the camp of the dwarfs? He finds the women of the village starting on an excursion after land-crabs.

"Would you like to go?" asks his mother.

CHAPTER XIII.

LAND-CRABS.

THE black men are very fond of the meat of the crabs, but they think it is woman's work to kill them. Mpuke is not so old, however, but that he is willing to go with his mother. It is great sport to get the crabs excited, and to see them, scuttling around, ready to attack their foes. Their anger is really amusing, and Mpuke is not the least bit afraid of them.

There are many kinds of these land-crabs. Some have beautiful red shells, while others are of a bright blue, but the ones best for eating are gray.

The party carry baskets and sharp knives, and, going down to the river, are soon paddling merrily along in their canoes. Mpuke entertains the women by singing a funny song, and mimicking the ways of the little dwarfs.

Hark! what is that slow, swishing sound of the water? It may be a herd of hippopotami bathing in the river. The women do not care to meet them, so they look anxiously ahead. They see the heads of the hippopotami reaching out of the water, but they are a long way ahead. They will reach the island where the land-crabs are found before they come too near the great beasts. The boats are soon drawn up on the low shore. Each one carries a knife and basket, and the hunt begins.

The feet sink into the black mud at every step, but there are no fine shoes to be spoiled, nor long dresses to hold up. The black women do not seem to be troubled by the difficult walking, for no harm can befall them.

Mpuke goes ahead, and is the first one to find traces of the crabs. He discovers a number of their burrows close together in the muddy soil. And, look! here comes an old grandfather crab to meet him. The old fellow brandishes one of his huge claws like a club, as if to say, "Don't dare to touch me, sir, or I'll knock you down."

Back of the old grandfather comes a whole army of crabs, some big, some little. There are fathers and mothers, aunts and uncles, children, and grandchildren. Some stand ready to fight, others run away in terror. Mpuke and the women are as busy as bees, chasing and catching their prey.

Watch our black cousin as he rushes upon this big crab. He strikes the back of the creature with a stout stick, and partially stuns it by the blow. At the same moment he seizes one of its great claws and tears it skilfully from the body. It is done in an instant, and Mr. Crab is now at his mercy.

But the next time Mpuke is not so successful. He strikes a good blow, but the crab manages to get away, and scuttles toward his own burrow. Mpuke springs forward, and knocks in his home, to the great amazement of the crab. What shall he do? Every moment is precious. He rushes to the burrow of a neighbour and tries to enter, but he is met by a pair of claws as big as his own.

"How dare you enter my house in such a rude manner?" perhaps the other exclaims, in crab language. His whole clumsy body follows the claws outside, and Mpuke holds his sides and laughs as the two crabs enter into a desperate fight.

At this moment there is a scream from one of the women. Her hand is held tightly in the claw of the crab she has attacked. Mpuke rushes up to her, and with one stroke of his knife cuts away the claw from the crab's body. But, even now, the hand is held tightly, for the muscles of the claw have not loosened their hold. The woman is faint with the pain, and keeps on screaming until the claw has been pried open, and her bruised hand bound in cooling leaves.

As for the crab, he hurries away as fast as possible to his own dark, quiet home. There he probably consoles himself with the thought that a new claw will grow in course of time, and take the place of the old one.

After an hour or two of busy work the baskets are filled, and the party make their way safely to their homes. There were no accidents, and not a single hippopotamus was seen.

The men are all home, and have great news to tell. Word has reached the village that white traders are coming this way. Every one is excited. The stores of ivory must be collected; the skins of the wild animals must be collected together; while Mpuke and his young friends will spend every spare moment in catching parrots and paroquets, and making cages for them. The traders may buy them to carry to children in far-distant lands.

Yes, Mpuke is delighted, above all else, that he may now be able to buy some beads for his precious mother.

Perhaps the traders will tell such stories of their own country that Mpuke will long to see it. It is even possible that they will grow fond of the black boy during their stay in this village, and will invite him to come to America with them. And perhaps he will accept the invitation. Who knows?

THE END.

Milton Keynes UK
Ingram Content Group UK Ltd.
UKHW012250290324
440241UK00004B/271

9 789357 955904